JOHN HANCOCK

JOHN HANCOCK

A Signature Life
Philip Koslow

A Book Report Biography
FRANKLIN WATTS
A Division of Grolier Publishing
New York / London / Hong Kong / Sydney
Danbury, Connecticut

Cover illustration by Mark Hess

Photographs © Archive Photos, 25; Corbis-Bettman, 12, 69; Harvard University Portrait Collection (Gift of John Hancock to Harvard College, 1766), 17; Library of Congress, 9; Jay Mallin Photos, 16, 55; National Portrait Gallery/Smithsonian Institution, 28; New York Public Library, 19, 22, 31, 44; North Wind Pictures, 2, 25, 33, 35, 39, 51, 62, 81, 89, 97

Visit Franklin Watts on the Internet at:
http://publishing.grolier.com

Library of Congress
Cataloging-in-Publication Data

Koslow, Philip.
John Hancock: A signature life / Philip Koslow
   p. cm.—(A Book report biography)
Includes bibliographical references (p.) and index.
Summary: Recounts the life of the colonial statesman, merchant, and patriot who became prominent during the American Revolution.
ISBN 0-531-11429-5
1. Hancock, John, 1737–1793—Juvenile literature. 2. Statesmen-United States—Biography—Juvenile literature. 3. United States. Declaration of Independence—Signers Biography Juvenile literature. 4. United States-History—Revolution, 1775–1783—Juvenile literature. [1. Hancock, John, 1737–1793. 2. United States—History—Revolution, 1775–1793.]
I. Title. II. Series.
   E302.6.H23K67   1998
   973.3'092-dc21
   [B]   97-12226
                                                       CIP
                                                        AC

CONTENTS

CHAPTER ONE

"PROCLAIM LIBERTY THROUGHOUT ALL THE LAND"

July 4, 1776, was a sunny and pleasant day in the city of Philadelphia, Pennsylvania. Even at the height of the afternoon, the temperature remained in the mid-70s, without a trace of the stifling heat that often blanketed the city in July. According to tradition, Andrew McNair spent this delightful afternoon sitting in the steeple of the imposing State House (now Independence Hall), looking out at the bustling city and the surrounding country-side. McNair, who had served nearly 20 years as the official doorkeeper of Pennsylvania's colonial legislature, would normally have been at his post down in the legislative chamber. But at this par-ticular moment, McNair's job was to stand by the massive 2,000-pound bell that had been shipped over from Great Britain in 1752. The smooth sur-face of the bell was broken by a jagged scar: it had cracked shortly after its arrival, and local ironsmiths had repaired it. Around the top of the bell, a verse from the biblical Book of Leviticus (25:10) was inscribed in the metal: "Proclaim liberty throughout all the land unto all the inhabitants thereof." For this reason, the bell was—and still is—known as the Liberty Bell.

When the Liberty Bell was first mounted in the steeple of the State House, the relationship between Great Britain and its American colonies was strong and harmonious. During the 1760s, however, these bonds became strained as the British government passed laws that many colonists found unfair and unjust. Tensions finally reached the breaking point in April 1775, when British troops clashed with colonial militiamen at Lexington and Concord in Massachusetts. Even though a state of war now existed, the colonies were still part of the British Empire, and Britain was offering forgiveness to Americans who laid down their arms. Since May 1775, the Second Continental Congress—made up of representatives from all 13 colonies—had been meeting in Philadelphia, debating the next step.

Many of the delegates had come to Philadelphia believing that a reconciliation was possible, but the movement for independence had grown swiftly. On July 2, the delegates had voted in favor of a declaration that would finally break the ties between the colonies and the mother country.

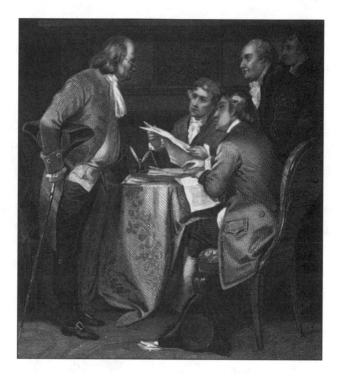

In the summer of 1776, Benjamin Franklin, Thomas Jefferson, Robert Livingston, John Adams, and Roger Sherman draft the Declaration of Independence.

Once the official document was drawn up and accepted by the Congress, there would be no turning back.

As the summer afternoon began to wane, a wild shout from below suddenly roused McNair. A young page had rushed excitedly from the hall.

"Ring! Ring!" he cried. McNair sprang into action and pulled the bell rope, making the clapper swing violently back and forth. The Liberty Bell thundered into life, pealing out over the city. Hearing its tones, the people of Philadelphia knew that the Declaration of Independence had been formally adopted—the American Revolution was on.

Moments before, the five-man committee in charge of drafting the declaration had presented their handiwork to John Hancock of Massachusetts, the handsome 39-year-old president of the Continental Congress. Written in flowing script on a large sheet of paper was the resolution created by Virginia's Thomas Jefferson. Its second paragraph contained these historic words:

We hold these truths to be self-evident, that all men are created equal; that they are endowed by their Creator with certain unalienable rights; that among these are life, liberty, and the pursuit of happiness. That, to secure these rights, governments are instituted among men, deriving their just powers from the consent of the governed; that, whenever any form of government becomes destructive of these ends, it is the right of the people to alter or abolish it, and to institute a new government, laying its foundation on such principles, and organizing its powers in such form, as to them shall seem most likely to effect their safety and happiness.

After specifying a long list of unjust acts committed by King George III and detailing unsuccessful attempts by the Americans to have their grievances heard, the declaration concluded:

We, therefore, the representatives of the United States of America, in general Congress assembled, appealing to the Supreme Judge of the world for the rectitude of our intentions, do, in the name, and by the authority of the good people of these colonies, solemnly publish and declare, that these united colonies are, and of right ought to be, free and independent states: that they are absolved from allegiance to the British crown, and that all political connection between them and Great Britain is, and ought to be totally dissolved. . . . And, for the support of this declaration, with a firm reliance on the protection of Divine Providence, we mutually pledge to each other our lives, our fortunes, and our sacred honor.

Taking up his quill pen, Hancock signed his name directly under the text, squarely in the center of

John Hancock's signature is the best known in U.S. history. As president of the Second Continental Congress, Hancock was the first delegate to sign the Declaration of Independence.

the sheet. Penmanship had been a point of pride with Hancock since his schooldays, and he had always inscribed his signature in large, well-formed letters, with an elegant flourish at the bottom. This time was no exception. "There!" he is said to have remarked when he finished writing. "King George III can read my name without his spectacles and may now double his reward of £500 on my head. *That* is my defiance."

"There! King George III can read my name without his spectacles and may now double his reward of £500 on my head."

Even after 55 other delegates had signed their names beneath the text, Hancock's signature remained the most striking feature of the

Declaration of Independence. No one could have missed it, with or without eyeglasses. As far as the British government was concerned, Hancock had boldly signed his own death warrant on July 4. By renouncing his allegiance to the British king, he had committed an act of treason, and the punishment for treason was death on the gallows. Hancock was fully aware of the risks, and so were his associates. At one point, Hancock remarked to the assembly, "We must be unanimous; there must be no pulling different ways; we must all hang together." Benjamin Franklin of Philadelphia, always ready with a witty remark, replied, "Yes we must indeed hang together, or most assuredly, we shall all hang separately."

AN UNLIKELY PATRIOT

Of all those who were putting their lives on the line for the cause of independence, Hancock may have been the most unlikely prospect. A highly successful businessman, he was one of the wealthiest men in the colonies. He lived in an elegant Boston mansion, drove through the streets in a magnificent carriage, sported the most fashionable clothing of any man in the colonies, and entertained on a lavish scale. He would gain nothing materially if the revolution succeeded, and if it failed he would swing from the end of a rope like a common criminal. Many men in his position were Loyalists (also known as Tories) who wished to preserve the connection to Britain at all costs. Some sincerely believed rebellion was wrong, but the majority simply wished to preserve their financial security and comfort.

Hancock had not only defied the odds by taking his stand with the revolutionaries. More remarkably still, he had been among the first men in the colonies to declare for liberty, and many historians believe that the revolution might not have succeeded without him. Yet throughout his life Hancock was often a controversial figure in his own country. As a leading citizen of Boston, he often performed magnificent acts of charity, for which he was deeply admired and loved by the common people. In private life he doted on his wife and the aunt who raised him, suffered keenly over the early death of his two children, and was generally kind and generous to his household servants. But many who dealt with him in politics thought him vain, bad-tempered, self-indulgent, calculating, and overly ambitious. In short, the author of the most famous signature in American history was a complicated man. The story of his eventful life reveals much about the powerful forces that brought the United States into being.

CHAPTER 2

THE MAKING OF A MERCHANT PRINCE

John Hancock was born on January 12, 1737, in Braintree, Massachusetts, a picturesque town nestled amid rolling hills a few miles south of Boston, the capital of the Massachusetts Bay Colony. Young John was the second child of John Hancock and Mary Hawke Hancock. He was born into a family that was highly respected though far from wealthy. John's father was the minister of Braintree's North Parish, and his grandfather, also named John, was a prominent minister in nearby Lexington. Both the elder Hancocks were graduates of Harvard College, the nation's first university, founded in 1636. It was understood that young John would follow his father and grandfather to Harvard when he came of age. After that, he would no doubt go on to become a man of the church.

At the age of five or six, John began his formal education at a dame school run by a Mrs. Belcher. The typical New England dame school was located in the home of a local schoolteacher, often an umarried woman. Here children learned the basics of reading, writing, and arithmetic. While he was still in dame school, John's comfortable childhood was soon disrupted by a tragic event. In the spring of 1744, when John was only 7 years old, his father died at the age of 41. In addition to this sudden blow, John also faced the loss of his home, because the parish house would be needed for the new minister hired to replace Reverend Hancock. Mary Hancock now had three children—the oldest, Mary, was two years older than John, and a second son, Ebenezer, had been born in 1741—and no means of income. When her father-in-law suggested that she and the children move into his house in Lexington, Mary gladly consented.

UNCLE THOMAS

As it turned out, John spent barely a year in Lexington before his uncle Thomas took a decisive hand in planning his future. Thomas Hancock had not followed his father and older brother into the ministry, mainly because the family did not have the money to send a second son to Harvard. At the age of fourteen, Thomas had been sent off to Boston, where he began working as an apprentice to a bookseller. By learning the arts of printing and binding—all done by hand in colonial times—Thomas could assure himself a living as an honest tradesman. Being an energetic and ambitious young man, he also took the opportuni-

In 1745, Thomas Hancock took in his young nephew John, whose father had died the previous year.

ty to make the acquaintance of the Boston merchants who visited his employer's shop.

Soon after Thomas finished his apprenticeship at the age of 21, he managed to set up his own bookshop in Boston. The shop did well, and four years later Thomas and three other merchants built a paper mill outside the city. After marrying Lydia Henchman (the daughter of one of his business partners) in 1731, he expanded his business dealings into other areas, including real estate, tea, and cloth. Thomas made money at everything he touched; by 1735, he was able to build a splendid stone mansion on Beacon Hill, then a grassy slope overlooking the Boston Common. (Built up during the early 19th century, Beacon Hill is now one of the most appealing historic neighborhoods in the United States.) The citizens of Boston recognized his achievements in 1739 when they chose him for the post of selectman. The Board of Selectmen governed Boston's affairs, subject to the approval of the colonial governor, and election to this body made Thomas Hancock one of the leading men of the city.

There was only one thing missing from Thomas Hancock's success story—he and his wife had never had children. When Thomas's brother died, the Boston Hancocks quickly offered to take John into their home. In this way, Thomas was not only promising his nephew a brighter future but also creating the possibility that a blood relative could inherit the powerful House of Hancock.

SCHOOL DAYS

Once he was settled into a large, comfortable room in his uncle's house, eight-year-old John was enrolled in the Boston Latin School. True to its name, the school emphasized the study of Latin

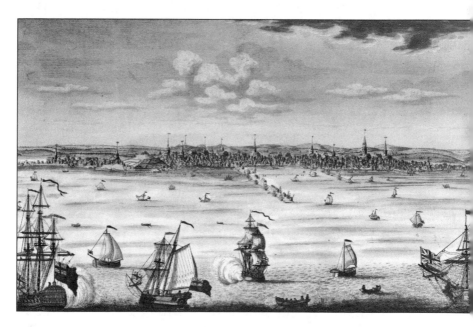

Boston Harbor teems with ships in the 1730s. John Hancock moved to the busy seaport when he was eight years old to live with his wealthy uncle and aunt.

and of the major works of ancient Greek and Roman literature. This was the foundation of a gentleman's education during the 18th century. Subjects such as arithmetic, spelling, and penmanship were left to more humble schools, which students attended at odd hours during the day. For example, John studied penmanship at a school run by Abiah Holbrook. He had a special talent in this area—under Holbrook's guidance, he learned to write an exceptionally fine script and developed the bold, elegant signature that was to become his trademark as a businessman and political leader.

By 1750, John Lovell, the headmaster at Boston Latin, felt that John had learned all he could at the school. Though John was barely more than 13, it was time for him to move on to Harvard, and he was readily admitted to the college on Lovell's recommendation. He entered Harvard as the second-youngest student in a freshman class of 20. Despite his youth, John's social standing assured him a number of privileges, including a choice of the best rooms. At the same time, he was subject to the restrictions imposed on all first-year students; among other things, he had to remove his hat whenever he met a senior and run personal errands for upperclassmen whenever he was asked.

The routine at Harvard was in many ways

unusual by modern standards. Students had to attend chapel every day at 6:00 A.M., and home-brewed beer was available for breakfast, along with biscuits, coffee, and chocolate. The main meal of the day consisted of meat and vegetables, washed down with cider that was drunk from a huge communal tankard. The college food was generally poor, and the wealthier students often took their meals elsewhere in Cambridge. Rich or poor, they were expected to keep at their books for hours on end, following the New England traditions of hard work and intellectual achievement. John continued to study Latin, Greek, and Hebrew and also took courses in mathematics and science. He was rated only an average student by Harvard standards. But he must have absorbed and retained a good deal because he was later considered among the most intellectual of the American patriots. During his sophomore year, John developed a reputation for indulging in drinking sprees at Cambridge taverns, and on one occasion he was severely reprimanded by the college authorities. He was certainly not following in the footsteps of his pious father and grandfather, and there was little chance that he would become the third Reverend John Hancock.

John received his bachelor's degree in July 1754. His mother, sister, and brother attended the Commencement Day ceremonies. That day

This illustration shows Harvard College as it appeared in the 1740s. John enrolled at Harvard when he was thirteen years old.

marked a parting of the ways for the Hancock family. John's grandfather had died two years earlier at the age of 81, but his mother was now well provided for; she had married a minister named Daniel Perkins and had moved to his home in the town of Bridgewater. In addition, John's sister was about to marry Richard Perkins, Daniel's son. Though John remained fairly close to his younger brother, Ebenezer, and eventually tried to set him up in business, he was to have little further contact with his mother and sister.

THE WORLD OF BUSINESS

After graduation, John returned to Beacon Hill and began to learn the basics of Thomas Hancock's business. Frequently, he went with his uncle to meet other merchants in taverns and coffeehouses, where most business deals were made. Now nearly a full-grown man, John was tall and slender, with carefully combed brown hair, dark eyes, a long, straight nose, and a firm chin. Like most well-bred men of the day, he covered his hair in public with a short white wig. In addition to the customary frock coat decorated with delicate gold embroidery and ruffles at the sleeves, John added many elegant and costly touches to his wardrobe.

As his earliest biographer, Abram English Brown, described him, "His shirt-front was trimmed with fine lace, and doubtless there was a great brooch stuck in it. His breeches were of green or red velvet, or white, lilac, or blue satin, and his fine shoes had the most expensive buckles." Before long, John was the undisputed fashion leader of New England. When he had his tailor make him a bright scarlet coat, the event caused a sensation—one country gentleman, a dedicated walker, is said to have hiked the 30 miles from Newbury to Boston just to obtain the cloth for a similar coat. However, Hancock was no idle fop. John Adams later recalled: "He became an example to all the young men of the town. Wholly devoted to business, he was as regular and punctual at his store as the sun in his course."

"He became an example to all the young men of the town."

—John Adams

In the summer of 1760, when John was 23, his uncle sent him on a business trip to London, the bustling center of the growing British Empire. Hancock spent a year abroad and apparently made the most of London's shops and taverns. In later years, it was rumored that he had a romance with a chambermaid during this interlude. At one point Uncle Thomas became concerned about the sums John was spending, and the young traveler was obliged to defend himself in a letter home:

> I am not Remarkable for the Plainess of my Dress, upon proper Occasions I dress as Genteel as any one, and can't say I am without Lace. I Endeavor in all my Conduct not to Exceed your Expectations in Regard to my Expences, but to Appear in Character I am Obliged to be pretty Expensive. I find Money some way or other goes very fast,

Luxurious carriages rattle through London's financial district. In 1760, Hancock traveled to London to transact business for his uncle's company.

but I think I can Reflect it has been spent with Satisfaction and to my own honour.

In fact, John accomplished quite a bit during his exciting year abroad, making a number of valuable contacts for the firm and securing an important contract for the supply of British troops in North America.

After John returned to Boston in 1761, Thomas Hancock became fully convinced that his nephew had the makings of a topflight businessman. In 1763, he made John a full partner in the House of Hancock. John immediately took hold, signing new contracts to supply British troops and involving the firm in the transport of whale oil from Nantucket, then a growing center of the whaling industry. Unfortunately, the whale oil venture yielded little profit at first, perhaps indicating that John still lacked his uncle's golden touch.

John's abilities would soon be put to the supreme test. Thomas Hancock, now in his early seventies, had been in poor health for some time. On August 1, 1764, he collapsed while attending a selectmens' meeting at the State House and had to be carried home and put to bed. Two hours later he was dead. John Hancock was now on his own.

CHAPTER 3

THE HOUSE OF HANCOCK

Thomas Hancock willed the Beacon Hill mansion and £10,000 to his wife, Lydia, and made generous provision for other relatives as well as a number of institutions, including Harvard and the Society for Propagating Christianity. But the bulk of the estate, including the House of Hancock, large parcels of land, and more than £60,000 in assets, went to John Hancock. Recognizing her nephew's position as head of the family, Lydia Hancock quickly signed the house over to John, asking only that she be allowed to live there for the rest of her life. John was more than happy to grant this wish, as he had long regarded the heavyset, kindly Aunt Lydia as his true mother.

At the age of 27, Hancock was now one of the wealthiest men in the American colonies. Not surprisingly, he was much in demand at dinners and other functions, and he often entertained guests

Lydia Hancock was like a mother to her nephew John.
When Thomas Hancock died, the bulk of his estate
went to John, who took control of the business and
took care of his beloved aunt.

at home. He showed no immediate desire to marry, however. For a time he seemed to be courting Sally Jackson, the daughter of a prominent Boston family, but Jackson ended up marrying someone else. Later on, he apparently developed a more casual relationship with Dorcas Griffiths, a buxom young widow who ran a tavern in one of Hancock's waterfront properties. This romance was clearly not headed for the altar, and Griffiths eventually took up with a British soldier and settled with him in London.

During this time, Hancock was deeply engrossed in his business affairs. Despite the wealth he inherited—his £60,000 would amount to many millions of dollars today—Hancock found himself operating under different conditions from those his uncle had known. Part of the problem was the return of peace to North America. From the 1740s to the early 1760s, the long, drawn-out war between Britain and France for control of Canada had brought the House of Hancock many lucrative contracts to supply British troops. In 1763, however, the Treaty of Paris granted Britain complete control of Canada, and military operations were drastically reduced. To make matters worse, the British government began looking for new sources of revenue to cover the costs of running their growing empire. Their solution was to levy taxes on the American colonies.

The first tax measure imposed by the British was the Sugar Act of 1764. This law actually reduced the tax on molasses, an important item throughout New England, but increased duties on other products and provided for more efficient methods of collection. American colonists, especially New Englanders, reacted angrily, denouncing the Sugar Act in meetings and legislative sessions. Many colonists vowed not to use a number of luxury items imported from Britain, including lace and ruffles. The first verbal shot in the American Revolution was fired at this time by James Otis. In a pamphlet entitled *The Rights of the British Colonies Asserted and Proved,* the Boston lawyer stated, "No parts of His Majesty's dominions can be taxed without their consent." This assertion highlighted one of the colonists' major complaints—although they were supposed to share the rights and duties of British citizens, they had no delegates in the British Parliament to represent their interests.

The Sugar Act affected merchants and smugglers more than the average citizen, and the uproar in the colonies might have simmered down in time if the British government had shown some tact and restraint. But in March 1765, George Grenville, first minister to King George III, put through an even more sweeping tax measure, the Stamp Act. This law decreed that colonists would have to purchase stamps from the British government and affix them to all legal documents, newspapers, college diplomas, and pamphlets—even to playing cards and dice. This tax would have an effect on almost everyone living in the colonies, regardless of social standing. To make matters worse, violators were to be tried without juries in

Under the Stamp Act of 1765, American colonists had to buy stamps such as this to paste on legal documents and other items.

British admiralty courts rather than in the local courts. The Stamp Act was to take effect on November 1, and as the weeks passed it was bitterly denounced by every newspaper in the colonies.

ENTERING POLITICS

The passage of the Stamp Act came only two weeks after Hancock's election as Boston's youngest selectman. His initial reaction, natural for a cautious merchant, was that the colonies would simply have to pay the new tax—after all, people in Britain had been paying it for many years. But when Virginia's legislature, the House of Burgesses, resolved that the colonists could only be taxed by their own assemblies, the debate took on a new dimension. In Boston, a newly created group called the Sons of Liberty held spirited meetings around the Liberty Tree, a massive 120-year-old elm in the center of the city.

"If the Stamp Act takes place we are a gone people."

After one of the August gatherings, a group of angry citizens destroyed a building belonging to Andrew Oliver, a merchant who was rumored to be the designated tax collector. Later in the month, another mob destroyed the home of Thomas Hutchinson, the lieutenant governor of Massachusetts. Hancock publicly denounced these assaults on the property of prominent citizens, but he sensed the tide of opinion in the colonies and began moving toward it. Writing on September 11 to the firm of Barnard and Harrison, his main business associates in London, he declared, "If the Stamp Act takes place we are a gone people." A month later, he was even more emphatic:

A group of colonists protest the Stamp Act. Widespread opposition to the tax persuaded Parliament to repeal the law in 1766.

I have come to a Serious Resolution not to send one ship more to Sea nor to have any kind of Connection in Business under a Stamp; . . . I would sooner subject myself to the hardest Labour for a maintenance, than carry on the Business I do now under so great a Burthen . . . . I am very sorry for this occasion of writing so boldly, & of being obliged to come to such Resolutions, but the Safety of myself & the Country I have the honour to be a Native of require some Resolutions, I am free & Determin'd to be so I will not willingly & quietly Subject myself to Slavery.

As a practical measure, Hancock joined 250 other New England merchants who agreed to fight back by refusing to import a long list of British-made products.

Colonial opposition had its effects in London. In the spring of 1766, the Stamp Act was repealed, and Boston erupted in celebration as the Sons of Liberty staged a fireworks display in Boston Common. Hancock hosted his own festivities, which included a banquet for his well-to-do friends, a barrel of wine for the general populace out on the Common, and more fireworks on the grounds of his estate. Shortly before, Hancock's opposition to the Stamp Act had won him election to the colonial legislature, known as the Massachusetts General Court. He had run with the solid backing of the Sons of Liberty and their fiery leader Sam Adams.

After the repeal of the Stamp Act, political passions cooled in Boston, and Hancock was free to concentrate on business. In 1767 he bought Boston's second-largest docking facility, soon to be known as Hancock's Wharf. He already owned

Sam Adams, leader of the Sons of Liberty, supported Hancock's election to the Massachusetts colonial legislature in 1766.

two ships, *Lydia* and *Boston Packet,* and had dreams of controlling an entire fleet of merchant vessels and dominating the transatlantic trade in whale oil. Politics, however, soon intruded on Hancock's personal affairs once again. A new crisis arose in 1767 when Charles Townshend, the newly appointed head of Britain's Exchequer (Treasury), announced a set of taxes on various items being imported by the colonies, including glass, paint, paper, and tea. In order to enforce these measures, the British Parliament granted sweeping new powers to colonial courts and officials, posing a serious threat to the personal liberties of the colonists.

Hancock and his fellow Bostonians reacted by pledging once again to limit their imports and to live more simply using homemade goods. Nothing more happened until February 1768, when the Massachusetts General Court issued a letter of protest against the new measures. This act stirred the emotions of the populace again, and in the following weeks, protesters threatened a number of officials who were designated to enforce the new regulations. When reports of this growing unrest reached London, Lord Hillsborough, secretary of state for the colonies, decided to take a hard line and show the colonists that Britain meant business. He decided to make an example of Hancock as a warning to the others.

In May, a cargo of wine was unloaded from one of Hancock's ships, *Liberty,* under cover of darkness, so that customs officials could not levy a tax on it. When the customs men realized what had happened, they boarded the ship and seized it. As *Liberty* was being towed into the harbor and secured to a British warship, an angry mob gathered on the wharf. The two customs officials in charge of the operation hastily retreated to their homes and barricaded the doors. The mob followed them and smashed their windows. Nothing could rescue *Liberty,* however, and the seizure of the ship promised to cost Hancock a good deal of money.

At first, Hancock was inclined to make a deal with the authorities in order to get his ship back, but after meeting with leaders of the Sons of Liberty he decided to stand on his rights and take the financial consequences. That decision cast him in the role of martyr to the cause of liberty. Hancock's name became a rallying cry, and his mansion was soon a a gathering place for Boston's leading patriots.

Hancock's prestige was reinforced when the *Liberty* case was heard in Vice-Admiralty Court during the summer. As expected, the judges ruled that the colonial government had a right to confiscate *Liberty* in order to make up for the tax revenue lost when the cargo disappeared. After refitting the vessel, the authorities sent it up and down the New England coast in search of smugglers. While *Liberty* was moored at Newport, Rhode Island, a group of local citizens stormed the ship and burned it.

THE REDCOATS

A new chapter in the gathering crisis unfolded in October 1768 when 1,200 British troops were dispatched to Boston from Halifax, Nova Scotia. After delicate negotiations with the citizenry, the red-coated soldiers were permitted to come ashore. Some set up temporary quarters in Boston's Faneuil Hall while others camped out on the Common, virtually on Hancock's doorstep. The presence of so many troops in a city of only 15,000 citizens was both a nuisance and a provocation. No one was more annoyed than Hancock, whose view of the Common was now spoiled by the jumble and hubbub of a military encampment, not to mention the odor of open latrines. It was a great relief to him when the soldiers were finally assigned to winter quarters in taverns and abandoned buildings throughout the city.

The point of having a powerful military force in Boston soon became clear. On November 2, the marshal of the Vice-Admiralty Court, knowing that no mob would dare to assemble with so many troops on hand, boldly marched up to Hancock's

Guests leave John Hancock's impressive stone mansion atop Beacon Hill. The Hancock home became a meeting place for Boston's leading patriots.

front door and handed him a summons to appear in court. This time the issue was the fate of the wine that disappeared from *Liberty*'s hold. If Hancock were convicted of smuggling, he would be liable to pay a fine of three times the value of the goods. This would amount to about £9,000 and would take a considerable bite out of Hancock's pocketbook. As it was, he had to post bail in the amount of £3,000 in order to avoid being jailed.

Hancock's trial dragged on for months. The prosecution had no actual proof of Hancock's involvement in the smuggling. Although they called a parade of witnesses to the stand, each one claimed to have no knowledge of what had happened to *Liberty*'s cargo. Hancock's attorney, John Adams, found the prosecution's case so weak that he complained of boredom. It was clear to Bostonians that the authorities were simply persecuting Hancock as a warning to other merchants.

Though it was far from their intention, they were also making Hancock a national hero, with the aid of a New York newspaper called the *Journal of the Times*. The paper was passionately anti-British and slanted its reporting of the trial to put the colonial authorities in the worst possible light. The *Journal* enjoyed a wide circulation, and Hancock was soon hailed throughout the colonies as a fearless defender of liberty. On March 25, the charges against him were finally dropped. The authorites felt that they had made their point. Hancock's business had suffered considerably while he was tied up in court, and other merchants would not be eager to have the same experience. On the other hand, the anti-British forces had a new hero to rally around, and Hancock's political fortunes were on the rise.

CHAPTER 4

BOSTON ON THE BOIL

By the time his trial was over, Hancock had become closely allied to Sam Adams, a fellow member of the General Court who was also John Adams's cousin. Though Adams and Hancock were both Harvard graduates and successful businessmen (Adams had inherited his father's brewery), they were otherwise vastly dissimilar in appearance and habits. Adams was a stocky, homely man who embraced the old Puritan ethic that condemned displays of wealth and lavish entertainments. Unlike Hancock, Adams lived in a modest house and was usually seen around town in the same well-worn suit of clothes. Whereas Hancock limited his social contacts to Boston's upper crust, Adams preferred the rough-and-tumble atmosphere of streets and taverns, where he rubbed elbows with men of all classes and created a vast network of political contacts. A brilliant orator and organizer, he provided much of the spark that drove the Sons of Liberty.

Despite their vast differences, Adams and Hancock were powerfully united by their opposition to the British government. Joining them in a sort of inner circle of opposition were two other Harvard men—James Otis, one of the sharpest lawyers in Boston, and the Reverend Samuel Cooper, the elegant minister of the Brattle Square Church, Boston's most fashionable place of worship. Other Sons of Liberty who were major actors in the cause included Dr. Benjamin Church, Joseph Warren, Thomas Young, and William Molineux.

THE BOSTON MASSACRE

The presence of the British troops was a constant irritant and rallying point for Boston's patriots. The Sons of Liberty accused the soldiers of committing rapes and other outrages and suggested that they were preparing to attack the citizenry. Not surprisingly, the "lobsterbacks" became favorite targets for physical and verbal abuse, and any citizen who asked a British officer to dinner was liable to be insulted and threatened by his fellow townsmen. The situation came to a head on March 5, 1770, when a group of dockhands—led by an African-American named Crispus Attucks, who occasionally worked for Hancock—began harassing the British sentry outside the Custom House on King Street. The soldier called for help, and 20 of his comrades arrived on the scene with fixed bayonets. For the next half hour, the soldiers confronted an angry mob of several hundred boys and men, who shouted insults and pelted the troops with snowballs packed with gravel and razor-sharp clam shells. Finally, one of the soldiers lost control and fired his musket. Several more shots rang out; when the smoke cleared, Attucks and two of his comrades lay dead, and two more men were mortally wounded.

Whoever was responsible for what came to be known as the Boston Massacre, the event played right into the hands of the Sons of Liberty. The following morning, Hancock himself led a delegation to the residence of Thomas Hutchinson, the acting governor, and demanded that the British troops be removed from Boston. Hutchinson agreed, and within a few days, the jubilant citizenry watched the hated redcoats board their longboats and retreat to Castle William, an island in Boston Harbor.

The governor's concession had little effect on the Sons of Liberty, who continued to express their outrage over the Boston Massacre. Adams and Cooper wrote lurid accounts of the event. The very title of Sam Adams's pamphlet, *Innocent*

The following text appears within the engraving:

The BLOODY MASSACRE perpetrated in King—Street BOSTON on March 5th 1770 by a party of the 29th REGT

BUTCHER'S HALL

Engrav'd Printed & Sold by Paul Revere Boston

uppy Boston! fee thy Sons deplore. | If fcalding drops from Rage from Anguish Wrung | But know Fate fummons to that awful Goal
hallow'd Walks befmear'd with guiltlefs Gore. | If fpeechlefs Sorrows lab'ring for a Tongue, | Where Justice ftrips the Murd'rer of his Soul
le faithlefs P—n and his favage Bands. | Or if a weeping World can ought appeafe | Should venal C—ts the fcandal of the Land
k murd'rous Rancor ftretch their bloody Hands; | The plaintive Ghofts of Victims fuch as thefe; | Snatch the relentlefs Villain from her Hand.
e fierce Barbarians grinning o'er their Prey; | The Patriot's copious Tears for each are fhed, | Keen Execrations on this Plate infcrib'd
prove the Carnage and enjoy the Day. | A glorious Tribute which embalms the Dead. | Shall reach a Judge who never can be brib'd

The unhappy Sufferers were Meff.ʳˢ Sam.ˡ Gray, Sam.ˡ Maverick, Jam.ˢ Caldwell, Chrispus Attucks & Pat.ᵏ Carr
Killed. Six wounded; two of them (Christ.ʳ Monk & John Clark) Mortally

On March 5, 1770, British soldiers fire into a Boston mob, killing five colonists. The Boston Massacre, as it became known, contributed to the unpopularity of the British rule.

Blood Crying to God from the Streets of Boston, was enough to arouse the fury of any patriotic American. As far as the Sons of Liberty were concerned, the Boston Massacre not simply a dockside brawl that got tragically out of hand—it was a calculated, cold-blooded act of savagery by the authorities. Eventually, Governor Hutchinson bowed to public pressure and ordered that a captain and nine soldiers be tried for murder. In a striking example of the colonists' passion for justice, the distinguished attorneys John Adams and Josiah Quincy defended the soldiers in court, winning acquittals for seven—the other two were convicted of manslaughter and branded on the hand by way of punishment.

When the General Court convened on March 15, Hancock and his allies pressed the attack against Governor Hutchinson, charging that his actions violated their rights as British subjects. The patriots' protests appeared to have an effect in London. On April 12, 1770, Lord North asked Parliament to repeal the hated Townshend Acts— except for the tax on tea. The tea tax would be kept in force to establish that Parliament was not giving up its taxing power but was rather showing indulgence to the colonists. This move had the desired effect, and colonial merchants announced that they were no longer going to shun British imports. Hancock refused to follow them, further increasing his stature as an uncompromising foe of British authority.

MAKING A NAME

Hancock's popularity was confirmed in August 1770 when he was elected moderator of the

Boston town meeting. As moderator, Hancock attempted to make peace with Governor Hutchinson. In 1772, Hutchinson made a friendly gesture by moving the meetings of the General Court from Cambridge to Boston, allowing Hancock to spend more time at home.

Hancock's public life at this time was not limited to business and politics. He also engaged in many acts of public philanthropy. For some years, he had been the foremost patron of Harvard, donating large sums to the college. In 1772, he contributed £1,000 for the building of a new Brattle Square Church and also presented the city with a new fire engine. Fire was a constant danger in American cities; most buildings were made of wood and heated by open fireplaces, and any stray spark from a hearth or chimney could create a fatal blaze. In 1760, a disastrous fire had destroyed 176 warehouses in Boston and wiped out 10 percent of the city's houses. A decade later, Boston had only six fire engines—crude pumping devices that were towed to the scene by firemen and operated by hand—and the city authorities were grateful to have another. The new engine was christened the "Hancock" and was stationed near Hancock's Wharf; the donor was granted the first claim on its use in case of fire.

Hancock also derived great prestige and pleasure from his role as commanding officer of the

Cadets, the city's militia. In addition to presiding over some jolly meetings at the Bunch of Grapes Tavern, Hancock took pains to see that the 80-man group received proper military training at weekly drill sessions. Not surprisingly, he also outfitted them with splendid uniforms that mirrored the British military fashion: red coats, white trousers, and beaver hats.

Hancock was feeling so relaxed in 1772 that he even took a summer vacation, sailing up to Maine with a small group of friends. By the end of this jaunt, however, political tensions in Boston began to rise again. The British had just announced that the salaries of Massachusetts' governor and Supreme Court judges were to be paid by London rather than by the local legislature. This was a direct slap at the colonists, removing any control they might have over their leading officials. The move inspired the formation of Committees of Correspondence throughout Massachusetts. In the committee meetings, outraged citizens vigorously confirmed their right to manage their own affairs. The situation was further inflamed when secret letters sent by Governor Hutchinson and his allies to a British minister were uncovered. In these letters, the Massachusetts officials attacked the Sons of Liberty and recommended that Britain gradually restrict the rights of the colonists. When the General Court convened in May 1773, Hancock led the delegates in calling for Hutchinson's removal.

TEA PARTY

Before any action was taken on this issue, an even more powerful crisis erupted over a common household item—tea. The problem began when Parliament stepped in to save the powerful British East India Company. Due to the continuing import tax on tea, American colonists were now boycotting the British product and smuggling in Dutch tea. The British could have solved this by simply abolishing the tea tax, but Lord North would not give in on this issue. He decided that the East India Company could undercut the Dutch by shipping directly to the colonies and selling through its own American agents, rather than dealing with a series of middlemen. North was convinced that American tea drinkers would be willing to pay the tax if they could save money at the same time.

Once again, North failed to grasp the attitude of the colonists. Those who hated the tea tax on principle were not going to be swayed by the chance to save a few pennies. In addition, many Americans feared that the British were now planning to gain a stranglehold on trade with the colonies. If the East India scheme proved successful, it might be extended to many other items, and American merchants would be out in the cold. To make matters worse, the five agents chosen by the East India Company included two of Governor Hutchinson's sons. The patriots called upon the agents to resign their commissions; when this demand was ignored, passions began to run dangerously high.

Between November 28 and December 7, three ships laden with East India Company tea arrived in Boston Harbor and tied up at Griffin's Wharf. Hancock quickly gathered a number of his militiamen, and the group stood guard at the wharf to make sure that none of the tea was unloaded. Hancock was resolute, declaring at one point that he was "willing to spend his fortune and life itself" to prevent the British from pushing through their scheme.

On December 16, 1763, the crisis came to a head. The first ship to arrive had been in the harbor for 20 days; according to law, the owners had to pay customs duties, or the tea would be brought ashore and sold by customs officials. With the moment of truth at hand, more than 7,000 Bostonians packed the Old South Church and its grounds. After some discussion, the meeting sent a delegate to Governor Hutchinson,

> **"Let every man do what is right in his own eyes."**

requesting that the ships and their cargo be sent back to England. When word of Hutchinson's refusal came, angry shouts and threats erupted from the assembled patriots. "Let every man do what is right in his own eyes," Hancock told the gathering. Sam Adams and his cohorts took it from there.

The events of that night were recounted by Hancock's friend John Andrews, who claimed to be an innocent bystander:

> They muster'd, I'm told, upon Fort Hill, to the number of about two hundred, and proceded, two by two, to Griffin's wharf, where Hall, Bruce, and Coffin [the ships] lay, each with 114 chests of the ill-fated article on board . . . and before nine o'clock in ye' evening, every chest from on board the three vessels was knocked to pieces and flung over ye' sides. They say the actors were Indians from Narragansett. Whether they were or not, to a transient observer they appear'd as such, being clothed in Blankets with the heads muffled, and copper color'd countenances, being each arm'd with a hatchet or axe, and pair pistols.

The Boston Tea Party, as it came to be known, was witnessed by a jubilant crowd of about 2,000. Neither Hancock nor Adams was among the "Indians," because they were considered too important to the cause to risk being arrested. However, the raiding party did include some prominent Sons of Liberty, including Will Molineux and Paul Revere. Though the loss of the tea was fairly minor, the Boston Tea Party was a major event. It was the first outbreak of organized, violent resistance to British rule, and it also placed the most radical colonists at the head of the protest movement. As the British government reacted to this event, it would soon become clear to Hancock and his fellow patriots that there was no turning back.

During the Boston Tea Party, a group of patriots dressed as Indians toss tea chests into Boston Harbor.

CHAPTER 5

THE REVOLUTION BEGINS

Hancock kept a low profile for months after the Boston Tea Party, in large part because he was suffering acutely from gout, an ailment that was to plague him on and off for the rest of his life. Caused by an excess of uric acid in the blood, gout often causes severe pain in the joints and can be extremely disabling. When Hancock was finally well enough to appear in public, he did so with tremendous effect. In recognition of his growing stature as a patriot, he was chosen as the speaker for the fourth annual Massacre Day observance, to be held in the Old South Church on March 5, 1774.

Hancock spoke for an hour before a packed crowd, and he lashed into Great Britain with a vengeance. Britain's rule, he exclaimed, was not a righteous government founded on principles of reason and justice but a brutal tyranny. He spoke of the evil effects of having British troops stationed on American soil, and when he came to recollecting the Boston Massacre, his passion and eloquence reached its crest. On that night four years earlier, he thundered, "Satan with his chosen hand open'd the sluices of New England blood, and sacrilegiously polluted our land with the dead bodies of her guiltless sons." One of the men wounded in the incident, Christopher Monk, was in the audience, and Hancock pointed him out: "Observe his tottering knees which scarce sustain his wasted body, look on his haggard eyes, mark well the deathlike paleness of his fallen cheeks and tell me does not the sight plant daggers in your souls?"

While the audience, deeply moved, began to pass the hat on behalf of the unfortunate Monk, Hancock warned that the enemies of liberty would be taking new measures: "Therefore let us also be ready to take the field whenever danger calls, let us be united and strengthen the hands of each other, by promoting a general union among us." To this end he proposed something no one had thought of before—a general congress made up of delegates from all the colonial legislatures in America. "At such a Congress," Hancock declared, " a firm foundation may be laid for the security of our Rights and Liberties; a system may be formed for our common safety."

Hancock's stirring speech—which Sam Adams and the other leading Sons of Liberty undoubtedly had a hand in writing—made him the talk of Massachusetts. When the speech was printed and circulated in Boston, four editions sold out in short order, and printers in the other colonies brought out their own editions.

"Therefore let us also be ready to take the field whenever danger calls, let us be united and strengthen the hands of each other, by promoting a general union among us."

Hancock, who loved the limelight, was no doubt thrilled by these developments. But he continued to suffer the ravages of gout, and business losses forced him to sell two of his ships. Though Hancock's vast fortune was in little danger of dissolving, it seemed that at the age of 37, he could expect little satisfaction outside of politics.

Aunt Lydia Hancock had different ideas. She thought it was high time her nephew found a wife. With this in mind, she invited a young acquaintance from Braintree, Dorothy Quincy, to make an extended visit to Beacon Hill. Dorothy, known as Dolly, was 10 years younger than Hancock. Though somewhat frail-looking, she was an intelligent and reasonably attractive young

Dolly Quincy met Hancock in 1775, and they married later that same year.

woman, and she had a reputation as a bit of a flirt. Her charms had a powerful effect on Hancock. Within a year he was deeply in love with Dolly, and it was understood that they would eventually marry.

TENSIONS MOUNT

Meanwhile, the British government was mulling over its response to the Boston Tea Party. Egged on by General Thomas Gage, commander of British forces in North America, the officials in London resolved to come down hard on their unruly colonial subjects. Between March and May, Lord North put forward a series of laws known as the Coercive Acts—measures that soon became known in New England as the Intolerable Acts.

The first law, the Boston Port Bill, decreed that the harbor would be closed to all commerce except military stores, food, and fuel until the East India Company was repaid for its lost tea. The Administration of Justice Act, passed in May, provided that any colonial official accused of a crime while pursuing his duties (such as putting down a riot) could be tried in Britain, thus removing him from the reach of colonial justice. The third law, the Massachusetts Government Act, struck at the very heart of colonial democracy. In this act Parliament decreed that members of the Massachusetts legislature would serve at the pleasure of the king and that all other leading officials—including juries—would be appointed by the colonial governor instead of being chosen by the people. In addition, town meetings in Massachusetts could be held only once a year and would be limited to business approved by the governor. Finally, the Quartering Act—which applied to all the colonies—provided that British troops would now be lodged in private homes as well as taverns and abandoned buildings. In order to show they meant business, the British authorities appointed General Gage the new governor of Massachusetts.

When the Boston Port Act took effect on June 1, Boston's economy went into a steep decline, leaving many of the city's workers idle. Still, the spirit of defiance ran high, and tension mounted during the summer. In October, the General Court convened (in Salem, the new capital of Massachusetts by order of Parliament), despite the opposition of Governor Gage. They proclaimed themselves the Provincial Congress and elected Hancock as their president. This was the first step in establishing an independent government in Massachusetts.

Throughout the fall and early winter, the Provincial Congress met at different locations in Massachusetts, including Concord and Cambridge. The legislators made several bold moves, including the demand that taxes be paid to Congress rather than the royal tax collectors. They also created a Committee of Safety, with Hancock as one of its leaders. Most important, they reorganized the colonial militia. Pro-British militiamen were expelled, and one-fourth of the remaining men were organized into 50-member companies that were ordered to be ready for action "at a minute's notice." These troops, known as the Minutemen, soon earned a lasting place in history. While the Committee of Safety made its preparations, the First Continental Congress, which included delegates from all the colonies, was meeting in Philadelphia and resolving to boycott all British imports.

As the winter wore on, the situation in Massachusetts grew increasingly volatile. In March, when the Provincial Congress met in Concord, Hancock and his fellow delegates made plans to form their own army, drawing up detailed rules for its organization and conduct. General Gage naturally viewed these developments with alarm. He regarded Hancock as one of the radicals' ringleaders, and there was a strong possibility that Hancock would be arrested if he returned to Boston. As a result, Hancock decided to spend some time in nearby Lexington. He was received as a welcome guest at his grandfather's old house, now occupied by Jonas Clarke, the pastor of Lexington's First Parish Church. Hancock found it too painful to remain apart from Aunt Lydia and Dolly Quincy, so the two women—along with Sam Adams, who was also in danger of arrest—came to stay in Lexington as well. The refugees from

Boston would soon find that their place of safety was right in the heat of the action.

LEXINGTON AND CONCORD

Informed by a spy that the colonials had a large store of gunpowder hidden in Concord, Governor Gage prepared to take swift action. He ordered the British troops to march on both Lexington and Concord—the two towns are only five miles apart—with a dual mission: to capture the powder and to seize Hancock and Adams. On the night of April 18, 1775, Gage sent 1,000 troops across the Charles, expecting them to reach Concord and Lexington under cover of darkness and do their work before the Americans could mount any resistance. However, the movement of the British forces was noticed by Boston's Committee of Safety. The committee dispatched two riders, Paul Revere and William Dawes, to alert the countryside. Revere reached Lexington in two hours and warned Hancock and Adams that the British were on their way.

Lexington's militia turned out in the early morning hours of the 19th, but as there was no sign of the British the men were sent home to bed. Shortly before dawn, a drumbeat sounded the alarm—the redcoats were on their way. Captain John Parker's company of Minutemen, 144 in number, quickly assembled on the Lexington Green. Hancock still considered himself a colonel in the militia—despite the pleas of Adams, Aunt Lydia, and Dolly, he hurried down to take command of the troops. Captain Parker, knowing that the Minutemen were badly outnumbered, convinced Hancock that he would only be shot or taken prisoner if he stayed. At this point, Hancock finally agreed to leave Lexington, and he and Adams took off for the north in a coach. There was no danger involved in leaving the women behind, as the rules of 18th-century warfare guaranteed their safety. Jonas Clarke, in a sermon he delivered the following year, described what happened next as the British troops appeared suddenly on the Green:

> Three officers advanced on horseback to the front of the body, and coming within five or six rods of the militia, one of them cried out, "Ye villians, ye rebels, disperse, damn you, disperse!" One of them . . . said, "Lay down your arms! Damn you, why don't you lay down your arms!" The second of these officers about this time fired a pistol towards the militia as they were dispersing. The foremost, who was within a few yards of our men, brandishing his sword and then pointing towards them, with a loud voice said to the troops, "Fire! By God, fire!"—which was instantly followed by a

discharge of arms from the said troops, succeeded by a very heavy and close fire upon our dispersing party, so long as any of them were within reach. Eight were left dead upon the ground! Ten were wounded. The rest of the company through divine goodness, were (to a miracle) preserved unhurt in this murderous action!

After scattering Parker's militiamen, the British marched on to Concord, where they captured what was left of the powder supply. (Much of it had been moved to safety two days earlier.) Later in the day, however, they were met by stiff resistance from militiamen defending Concord's North Bridge. After suffering 14 casualties, the British withdrew from Concord and began a long retreat back to Boston. But the countryside was now teeming with militiamen, who fired on the British from the cover of trees, rocks, and stone fences along the entire line of march. If not for the arrival of reinforcements outside Lexington, the British force might have been annihilated. As it was, they suffered 73 killed and 174 wounded before reaching the safety of Boston, where the heavy guns of their warships made further pursuit suicidal. The Americans suffered a total of 93 casualties for the day.

In recounting the action at Lexington, the British authorities insisted that one of the Min-

On April 19, 1775, British troops open fire at colonial militiamen at Lexington, Massachusetts. The Battle of Lexington and Concord stirred up support for the cause of independence.

utemen had fired the first shot and that the British troops had merely acted in self-defense. Historians have never been able to determine whether or not this is true. In any case, it was the American version—forcefully expressed by Jonas Clarke and others—that circulated throughout the colonies. Convinced that Americans had been wantonly fired upon as they were obeying the order to disperse, thousands of outraged citizens now rallied to the cause of independence—even in the South, where pro-British feeling had always run high. The American Revolution was now a reality.

CHAPTER 6

FIGHTING FOR FREEDOM

Only a few hours after the Battle of Lexington, Hancock was reunited with Aunt Lydia and Dolly at the town of Woburn. From there they all headed for Philadelphia, where Hancock, Adams, and the other Massachusetts delegates were to attend the Continental Congress. While crossing Connecticut, the party made a stop in Fairfield, where Dolly and Aunt Lydia were installed in the home of an old family friend.

On May 6, the Massachusetts delegates arrived at New York City. They received a hero's welcome, which Hancock described in a May 7 letter to Dolly: "When we Arriv'd within three Miles of the City we were met by the Grenadier Company and Regiment of the City Militia under Arms, Gentlemen in Carriages and on Horseback, and many Thousands of Persons on Foot, the Roads fill'd with people, and the greatest Cloud of Dust I ever saw." More than 7,000 citizens (one-third of the population) filled the streets as the procession entered the city. Hancock's carriage was given the honor of being the first in the procession. When the crowd caught sight of him, they pressed around the carriage and began to unhitch the horses, meaning to pull the vehicle through the streets themselves. Hancock told Dolly that he prevented this excessive display of hero worship, but considering his well-known love of ceremony he must have been highly gratified. When he reached his lodgings, he was securely guarded by militiamen as a steady stream of well-wishers came to speak with him. It was ten o'clock at night before he even had a chance to enjoy his supper of fried oysters.

THE CONTINENTAL CONGRESS

Four days later, Hancock's party reached Philadelphia, where another cheering throng awaited, and the Second Continental Congress opened for business immediately. The session included delegates from all of the 13 colonies except Georgia, which did not take part until the second session. Delegations consisted of two to five members, but each colony had only a single vote. The delegates' first act was to select Peyton Randolph of Virginia, who had headed the First Continental Congress, to continue as president. When Randolph was called home to preside over the House of Burgesses, the delegates turned to Henry Middleton of South Carolina, who declared that his poor health would not permit him to serve. Political fairness suggested that the delegates then consider a northerner. Hancock—combining social position, political experience, and celebrity status—was the unanimous choice.

On June 10, the Congress took its first major action by assuming command of the 10,000 militiamen who were encircling Boston, keeping the 6,500-man British garrison hemmed in. The militia was now to be known as the Continental Army, and Congress made provision for six more companies of riflemen from surrounding colonies to reinforce the troops in Boston. On June 15, the delegates chose Virginia's George Washington as commander of the Continental Army. Before Washington could take up his post, however, the fighting men were severely tested. On June 17, British forces crossed the Charles and assaulted the American fortifications on Breed's Hill. Marching in tight formation and carrying heavy packs, they made two successive charges but were driven back by intense fire from rifles and cannon. At this point the British commander, Sir William Howe, ordered his men to drop their packs and make a bayonet charge. The Americans were running low on powder, and the British took the hill on the third attempt; with Americans forces in full retreat, the British swept on to capture nearby Bunker Hill. Though technically a British victory, the Battle of Bunker Hill, as it came to be known, provided a boost for the American cause. The British had suffered 1,054 casualties to only 367 for the Americans, in what turned out to be the bloodiest encounter of the American Revolution. When Washington arrived in Cambridge on July 3 to take command of his troops, there was reason to believe that he had a fighting force equal to the cream of the British army.

Despite their military confidence, most Americans had not yet embraced the idea of all-out war. After some debate the delegates agreed on July 5 to offer Britain the Olive Branch Petition. In this document, the Congress indicated that the American people were still loyal to King George III and asked him to prevent further military action until some agreement could be worked out. On the following day, Congress issued its Declaration of the Causes and Necessities of Taking Up Arms, assuring Britain that "we mean not to dissolve that union which has so long and so happily subsisted between us." Americans, however, would continue to fight "in defense of that freedom that is our birth-right" and "for the protection of our property, acquired solely by the honest industry of or fore-fathers and ourselves." Americans would lay down their arms, the declaration stated, "when hostilities shall cease on the part of the aggressors." Before adjourning on August 2, Congress appointed commissioners to negotiate peace treaties with Indian tribes and set up a Post Office Department, with Benjamin Franklin of Philadelphia as the first postmaster general. Though hoping for reconciliation, Americans were purposefully taking control over their own affairs.

MARRIAGE

Hancock took advantage of the break to visit Fairfield. He had missed Dolly terribly while in Philadelphia. To make matters worse, she did not enjoy writing and rarely did so. (To date, scholars have failed to unearth a single letter written in her hand.) "I beg, my Dear Dolly," Hancock had written in June, "you will write me often & long Letters, I will forgive the past if you will mend in future." This plea produced no result. Hancock realized that the only way he would hear from Dolly was to have her at his side, and he now urged that they be married as soon as possible. Dolly readily agreed, and the couple were wed on August 28 by Reverend Andrew Eliot. In better times, the wedding would certainly have been a lavish affair. But with struggle and sacrifice facing the colonies, simplicity was the order of the day. Meanwhile, Hancock's business affairs were entirely disrupted by the situation in Boston—there were rumors that British officers were casting lots to see who would take over his properties.

PRESIDENT OF THE CONGRESS

When the Continental Congress reconvened, the Hancocks were settled into a comfortable house in Philadelphia. Hancock resumed his duties as president and also served as the head of the Marine Committee, whose task was to create a Continental Navy and two battalions of marines. His gout continued to torment him, however, and he also faced a moderate crisis in September when Peyton Randolph returned from Virginia. Many delegates assumed that Hancock would offer to step aside and allow the tall, portly Virginian to resume the presidency. But Hancock showed no sign of making such a gesture. A number of his colleagues, including Sam Adams, thought Hancock's ego was getting out of hand. The issue might have come to a head at some point, but Randolph solved the problem by dying unexpectedly.

In addition to building up the armed forces, making peace with Native Americans, and borrowing funds, the Second Continental Congress also took steps to contact potential allies in Europe, particularly the French. As the winter

COMMON SENSE:

ADDRESSED TO THE

INHABITANTS

OF

AMERICA.

On the following interesting

SUBJECTS.

I. Of the Origin and Design of Government in general, with concise Remarks on the English Constitution.

II. Of Monarchy and Hereditary Succession.

III. Thoughts on the present State of American Affairs.

IV. Of the present Ability of America, with some miscellaneous Reflections.

Written by an ENGLISHMAN.

By Thomas Paine

Man knows no Master save creating HEAVEN,
Or those whom choice and common good ordain.

THOMSON.

PHILADELPHIA, Printed

And Sold by R. BELL, in Third-Street, 1776.

The title page of Thomas Paine's Common Sense. *The pamphlet convinced many colonists that independence was their true goal.*

came on, the likelihood of a peaceful settlement with Great Britain was looking more and more remote. In November, Parliament rejected the Olive Branch Petition as a basis for reconciliation, and on December 23, King George issued a royal proclamation closing the American colonies to all overseas trade. In the colonies, calls for independence became even stronger after January 1776, when Thomas Paine published his influential pamphlet *Common Sense.* Paine, born in the same year as Hancock, was an equally intriguing character. The son of a corsetmaker, Paine had come to the colonies from England only in 1774, but he adopted the colonial cause as his own. "Where liberty is, there is my country," he declared.

Having failed to make a living at a variety of trades, Paine now found his calling as a revolutionary journalist. In *Common Sense,* he condemned George III as "a crowned ruffian" and dubbed him the Royal Brute of Britain. Paine argued that it was only "common sense" for the colonies to separate themselves from the rule of such a corrupt monarch, who had compelled them to fight in his wars and had then trampled on their liberties. In one of his most stirring passages, Paine cried out to Americans, "O! ye that love mankind! Ye that dare oppose not only the tyranny but the tyrant, stand forth!" *Common*

Sense was a runaway success, selling 120,000 copies in three months and playing a major role in priming the colonies for full-scale rebellion.

No less energetic than Paine, Hancock threw himself into the work of the Congress, which met six days a week. The sessions began at seven in the morning and usually lasted until ten at night, with breaks for lunch and supper. As president, Hancock had an even heavier workload than the other delegates. He had many official letters to write and was also expected to sign every document relating to the work of the Congress. In order to deal with the oceans of paperwork, Hancock often employed private secretaries at his own expense.

BACK TO BOSTON

The British evacuated Boston in March 1776. Much to his relief, Hancock learned that his mansion was largely unharmed, mainly because one of the British commanders, General Henry Clinton, had used the house as his headquarters. However, a number of Hancock's commercial properties had been destroyed or badly damaged—his total losses amounted to some £6,000. The city as a whole had also suffered considerable damage, ranging from leveled buildings to petty acts of revenge. For example, the British had cut down the Liberty Tree—in the process, one soldier was killed by a falling limb—and had also effaced Hancock's name from the cornerstone of the Brattle Square Church.

When Hancock returned to Boston, the General Court raised his rank in the militia from colonel to major general, an honor never conferred on any other citizen. This was highly gratifying to Hancock, especially as his relations with Sam Adams were deteriorating. During the preceding months, Adams had become more and more disgusted with what he saw as Hancock's lust for personal honors, his high style of living in Philadelphia, and his coziness with the richer, more conservative members of Congress. By the time the session ended, the former allies were barely speaking to one another.

If Hancock regretted the loss of Adams as a friend, he suffered a greater blow in April when Aunt Lydia Hancock was felled by a stroke. For a short time she appeared to recover but then took a turn for the worse and died on the 25th. Both John and Dolly were grief-stricken. They had loved Aunt Lydia dearly and regretted that the press of official business had made it impossible to visit her since their wedding. Dolly was now pregnant, and the Hancocks had hoped that Aunt Lydia would come to Philadelphia to help Dolly manage the household. As that was no longer possible, Dolly's older sister, Catherine Quincy, agreed to come and lend a hand.

DECLARING INDEPENDENCE

All these personal events were the prelude to a summer filled with historic events. The desire for independence was gaining ground throughout the colonies, and citizens were urging their delegates to place the issue before the Congress. On June 7, 1776, Virginia's Richard Henry Lee offered the following resolution: "That these united colonies are, and of right ought to be, free and independent states; that they are absolved from all allegiance to the British crown and that all political connection between them and the state of Great Britain is and ought to be totally dissolved."

Congress decided to wait until July 1 for a vote on this issue. Meanwhile, the delegates appointed a Committee of Five—Thomas Jefferson of Virginia, John Adams of Massachusetts, Benjamin Franklin of Pennsylvania, Robert R. Livingston of New York, and Roger Sherman of Connecticut—to draft a document presenting the arguments for independence. The committee members chose Jefferson to do the actual writing. He completed his draft of the document in late

June, and it was submitted to the Congress for review. The delegates wanted two major changes, as Jefferson recalled in his autobiography:

The pusillanimous [cowardly] idea that we had friends in England worth keeping terms with, still haunted the minds of many. For this reason, those passages which conveyed censures on the people of England were struck out, lest they should give them offence. The clause too, reprobating the enslaving the inhabitants of Africa, was struck out in complaisance to South Carolina and Georgia, who had never attempted to restrain the importation of slaves, and who, on the contrary, still wished to continue it. Our northern brethren also, I believe, felt a little tender under those censures; for though their people had very few slaves themselves, yet they had been pretty considerable carriers of them to others.

Thus amended, the Declaration of Independence received Hancock's historic signature on July 4. It was printed overnight by John Dunlap, and the process of circulating it throughout the colonies began. In Philadelphia, the declaration was read aloud on the Common on July 8, followed by a

John Hancock signs the Declaration of Independence. His defiance against the British king was an act of treason, punishable by death.

jubilant celebration that included bonfires, fireworks, and the ringing of all the bells in the city. On July 9, General Washington received his copy of the declaration in New York and read it before his troops. The New York chapter of the Sons of Liberty promptly pulled down a lead statue of King George and prepared to melt it down for the manufacture of bullets. In Dover, Delaware, a portrait of the king was burned in the public square, and later in the month a Connecticut infant was baptized with the name Independence.

However, jubilation soon gave way to gloom when Americans learned that their army was not as strong as they had thought. In late August, a powerful British force under Sir William Howe landed in Brooklyn (then known as Long Island) and set upon Washington's troops. The British drove the Continentals out of Long Island and pursued them across Manhattan and New Jersey, stopping only when Washington's men took refuge on the Pennsylvania side of the Delaware River. To make matters worse, the British occupied New York and put the city to the torch, destroying more than 300 buildings. The only bit of good news was France's decision to back the American cause. Before long, American delegates would be in Europe to arrange loans and purchase war supplies. In September, Hancock issued an appeal to all the 13 colonies, rallying those who might be discouraged by the military situation:

> Let us convince our enemies that, as we are entered into the present contest for the defense of our liberties, so we are resolved, with the firmest reliance on Heaven for the justice of our cause, never to relinquish it,

but rather to perish in the ruins of it. If we do but remain firm . . . and are determined, at all hazards, that we will be free—I am persuaded under the gracious smiles of Providence, assisted by our own most strenuous endeavors, we shall finally succeed . . . and thereby establish the independence, the happiness, and the glory of the United States of America.

CHAPTER 7

VICTORY

During the winter of 1776–77, no one needed encouragement more than Hancock himself. Even though Dolly gave birth to a daughter, Lydia Henchman Hancock, in November, the rest of the news was all bad. The British were threatening to invade Philadelphia, and the members of the Continental Congress voted to abandon the city and set up a temporary capital in Baltimore. The 100-mile trip was extremely difficult, as the winter weather turned the dirt roads into seas of mud. When the Hancocks finally arrived in Baltimore, they found that lodgings were very expensive and well below their standards of comfort. When it became clear that Philadelphia was not in danger, Congress took heart and decided to reconvene there in March. Not wishing to uproot his family again, Hancock went up alone, and in the coming weeks he suffered keenly from the separation: "I lead a doleful lonesome life," he complained to Dolly at one point. When Dolly finally did join her husband, she found life in Philadelphia more and more unsatisfactory and finally went back to Boston with the baby. Tragically, little Lydia became ill and died during the summer, an all too common occurrence in that time, when the art of medicine was crude even for the wealthy. Grieving and in pain from his gout, Hancock longed to give up the responsibilities of office and return home.

"I lead a doleful lonesome life."

There was more bad news in September 1777, when the British defeated Washington's forces at the Battle of Brandywine Creek. Two weeks later they marched on Philadelphia, forcing Congress to evacuate once again—this time to York, Pennsylvania. In October, Washington engaged the British at Germantown but failed to push them back. But the Americans got a great boost on October 13 when General Horatio Gates defeated a British force under General John Burgoyne at Saratoga, New York. This was a smashing victory for the United States: 5,700 British troops laid down their arms, prepared themselves for shipment home, and promised to take no further part in the war. Seizing this positive moment, Hancock informed the Congress that he was taking a two-month leave of absence. After a long and uncomfortable journey, he finally reached Boston on November 19. Much to his delight, his carriage was met by a cheering crowd that included all the local militia units.

HARD TIMES

Hancock's mansion had survived the ravages of war, but the same could not be said of his business affairs. His principal agent, William Bant, had been forced to sell off the remaining ships, and there was no longer any chance of Hancock's operating as a transatlantic merchant. He now had to rely on rental income from his real estate holdings and his salary as a public official. From here on, Hancock trusted Bant to look after the business, while he himself concentrated on politics. He was still a wealthy man and continued to live in high style, riding through the streets in a splendid carriage manned by liveried servants. He also kept up his charitable donations, which included firewood for the poor and financial aid to the families of men serving in the army. Hancock was now the most popular man in Massachusetts by a wide margin—much to the annoyance of Sam Adams, who bitterly remarked that Hancock's admirers were "asses and slaves."

Despite the great victory at Saratoga, the

winter of 1777–78 was a desperate time for the American cause. Washington's troops, hemmed in at Valley Forge, Pennsylvania, were woefully short of supplies and warm clothing; 2,500 men died of cold and hunger, and many more deserted. The outlook brightened in February 1778, however, when France entered into a formal alliance with the United States, promising monetary aid and military support. At this point, Hancock felt

During the harsh winter of 1777–78, Washington's troops try to stay warm in their Valley Forge camp.

that he had done all he could as a member of the Continental Congress and could do more good by staying in Boston. But a number of delegates were grumbling about his long absence, and he made up his mind to return. He delayed his departure until late spring because Dolly was expecting again, and he did not wish to be away if anything went wrong. Happily, Dolly gave birth to a healthy boy on May 21, 1778; the child was christened John George Washington Hancock.

When Hancock returned to Congress, eight months had gone by since he took his leave. Henry Laurens of South Carolina had been elected president in Hancock's absence, and Laurens showed no sign of stepping down. Hancock had to accept the situation, and his enemies were pleased to see him get a dose of the medicine he had given to Peyton Randolph in 1775. Bored with the routine work at hand and lonely for his family, Hancock still managed to enjoy the gala dinner celebrating the second anniversary of the signing of the Declaration of Independence. Soon afterward, the first French ambassador to the United States, Conrad Alexandre Gérard, arrived in Philadelphia. Gérard had been transported across the Atlantic by a fleet of French warships, and this force was eager to engage the British.

With support from the French fleet, American forces under General John Sullivan prepared to assault the British garrison occupying Newport,

Rhode Island. Sullivan called for 5,000 militiamen from New England, and Hancock, as major general of the Massachusetts militia, was only too happy to hurry back home and assume command of his troops. Much to the Americans' dismay, the French commander, Count Giscard d'Estaing, decided to withdraw his ships to Boston after several of them were damaged by a sudden storm. There was no way to assault Newport without massive naval support, and the militiamen quickly disbanded.

When Hancock returned to Boston, he set about entertaining d'Estaing and his officers in fine style at Beacon Hill—on one occasion, 150 Frenchmen unexpectedly showed up for breakfast, and the servants scurried about town rounding up provisions to feed them all. French gold did much to restore Boston's prosperity, and just before these well-heeled allies sailed off on November 3, Hancock threw a lavish ball in their honor at the Concert Hall. Predictably, this display of wealth and finery drew harsh criticism from Hancock's opponents, who saw it as an insult to the many citizens suffering privations during the war.

GOVERNOR HANCOCK

Realizing that he would never again be president of the Continental Congress, Hancock had no intention of returning to Philadelphia. Massachusetts was in the process of drafting a new constitution, and Hancock had his heart set on the governorship. The first election under the new charter was held in the fall of 1780, and Hancock polled more than 90 percent of the vote. To make his victory even sweeter, his friend Thomas Cushing was chosen lieutenant governor.

Hancock's October 25 inauguration took place at Boston's State House and was followed by a celebration at Faneuil Hall. A few days later, the new governor addressed the General Court and announced that his first priority was to win the war. He proposed new measures to build up the army and called for a law to lengthen the enlistment period for soldiers, many of whom served for brief periods and returned to their farms when it was time for planting and harvesting. As governor, Hancock was diligent in seeing that Massachusetts fulfilled its quota of men and supplies for the Continental Army.

As the war dragged on, America's citizen-soldiers made steady progress against the world's most powerful army. After 1779, Massachusetts and the rest of the Northeast were free of fighting while the British devoted all their resources to conquering the South. This attempt came to a disastrous end on October 19, 1781, when Lord Charles Cornwallis, surrounded by American and

French forces at Yorktown, Virginia, ordered his troops to lay down their arms. When the news reached Boston, the city erupted in a wild celebration. After more than six years of war, the British were beaten. Though the formal peace treaty was not signed until 1783, the cause to which Hancock had sacrificed his health and his business had finally triumphed.

Now that the war was over, Hancock's first concern was to put his business affairs in order. His agent William Bant had died in 1780, and Hancock had not found anyone to replace him. As a result, Hancock had forfeited more than 20,000 acres of real estate by failing to pay taxes, and various debtors owed him about £12,000. Undismayed, Hancock hired a new agent to collect the money owed him. He continued to live in high style, purchasing silverware, furniture, carpets, and a new carriage. Here and there he made a concession to practicality; in one of his letters he confided that he really preferred the more humble pewter plates (made of tin and lead) to silver—the food did not slide off them, and there was less annoyance from the clatter of knives and forks.

Despite continued sniping by his critics, Hancock easily won reelection as governor in 1781, 1782, 1783, and 1784. During this time, however, he did little to address the severe problems facing Massachusetts. The state's shipping and fishing industries had been badly disrupted by the war, and trade with the British Empire was now out of the question. Farmers were suffering from high taxes and heavy interest rates on the money they owed, and merchants complained that they could not compete against a glut of foreign goods. Hancock proposed no remedies for these ills, and in the eyes of Sam Adams's faction he made things worse by encouraging more prosperous citizens to flaunt their wealth.

As the 1785 election approached, Hancock suddenly resigned, probably more due to ill health than the fear that he would be voted out of office. He counted on the loyal Thomas Cushing to win the election and hold the governor's chair until he was ready to return. But Cushing was upset during the election by James Bowdoin, one of Adams's men. Hancock had been thwarted for the first time in his political career, but he was far from finished with public life.

CHAPTER 8

FORGING A NATION

Hancock remained a private citizen for two years, occupying himself with business matters. During this time, discontent grew rapidly in western Massachusetts. The impoverished farmers of the region found an impassioned leader in Daniel Shays, a former captain in the Continental Army. Shays organized a large group of followers, many of them fellow war veterans, and demanded a number of reforms: Chief among them were tax relief, a grace period on debts, and abolition of debtor's prison. During the summer of 1786, Shays and his men took up their rifles and traveled the countryside, shutting down courts that were hearing suits for debt collection. Suddenly, the former rebels now serving in the state legislature found themselves defending the established order. Sam Adams and his followers denounced Shays as a traitor, and a group of Boston merchants raised the money to finance a large-scale militia expedition to the west.

The issue came to a head in January 1787, when Shays and 1,200 of his men attempted to storm the arsenal at Springfield in order to obtain more weapons. The militia were waiting for them and drove them off after killing four men. In a final showdown on February 3, the militia attacked Shays's force at Petersham and captured 150 men. The rest scattered, and Shays himself fled to Vermont. He and two other leaders were later pardoned for their actions, but they actually achieved some of their immediate goals when the legislature canceled tax collections for 1787 and passed laws granting some relief to those in debt.

In the midst of Shays's Rebellion, the Hancock family suffered its own private tragedy. Like most New England children, young John Hancock, now nine years old, was an avid skater. While enjoying his skates on a local pond one January day, he fell and hit his head hard on the ice. He was brought home unconscious and died a short time later. On the day of the funeral, John's coffin was carried to the cemetery in the family coach, while the grief-stricken parents walked behind. A number of John's schoolmates were in the funeral procession. Some had written poems mourning his loss, and they read these verses at the gravesite. For the second time, John and Dolly

In January 1787, Daniel Shays and his followers attempt to seize the arsenal at Springfield, Massachusetts.

Hancock had lost their only child. They continued to mourn intensely for many weeks, as evidenced by a letter Hancock wrote in mid-March to General Henry Knox, one of the heroes of the revolution: "As my situation is totally deranged by the untimely death of my dear and promising boy, I have no affectionate object to promise myself the enjoyment of what I leave."

> **"As my situation is totally deranged by the untimely death of my dear and promising boy, I have no affectionate object to promise myself the enjoyment of what I leave."**

Fortunately for Hancock's state of mind, he was soon back in the political arena. Massachusetts' citizens, weary of the turmoil that had wracked the state during Hancock's absence from the State House, looked to their former governor for relief: he had always advocated stability, yet he had not been part of the anti-Shays movement and would not seek reprisals against the defeated rebels. In the spring the voters rejected Bowdoin and elected Hancock governor by a three-to-one margin. To make sure that harmony had been restored to Massachusetts, Hancock made a personal tour of the western counties during the summer.

A MORE PERFECT UNION

In addition to providing temporary relief for the have-nots, Shays's Rebellion also helped to convince many Americans of the need for a strong central government. Since 1781, the states had been bound together by the Articles of Confederation. Under this arrangement, Congress was the only branch of the U.S. government, and all major decisions had to be made with the approval of 9 out of 13 states. It soon became clear, however, that Congress really had no way of enforcing its decisions; it had trouble raising money; and foreign governments had little confidence that the central government could speak for all the states. By 1786 new ideas were in the wind for the creation of a stronger union. To this end, a constitutional convention convened at Philadelphia's State House in May 1787.

Hancock's duties as governor prevented him from attending the convention, but those who did included many of the nation's most eminent figures: George Washington, Benjamin Franklin, James Madison, George Mason, Roger Sherman, and Gouverneur Morris were among the leaders of the discussions. A number of different plans for organizing a new government were put forward and debated. In mid-September, the delegates agreed on the draft of a new constitution that would create a government with three separate branches. In addition to Congress there would be a president who had the power to speak for the nation, command the armed forces, and negotiate with foreign powers; there would also be a system of federal courts, headed by the Supreme Court, to settle disputes between citizens of different states or between the states themselves.

As governor of Massachusetts, Hancock received the proposed constitution and presented it to the General Court for approval. He made no official statement of his personal opinion, but the indications are that he was not in favor of adoption. As a longtime advocate of home rule, Hancock was reluctant to see Massachusetts surrender any of its powers to a new central authority. He was also unhappy that the proposed constitution lacked a bill of rights safeguarding individual liberties. Sam Adams felt the same way, marking the first time in several years that he and Hancock were on the same side of an issue. Because of Massachusetts' stature as a leader of the revolution, its decision would have a powerful effect on the rest of the colonies. If the Bay State voted no, the constitution was most likely doomed.

Hancock was chosen as one of Boston's 12 delegates to the Massachusetts ratifying convention, which began on January 2, 1788. The convention elected Hancock to sit in the president's chair, though his poor health forced him to miss many of the sessions. When the discussions got under way, there was a fairly even balance between the generally conservative Federalists, who favored the new constitution, and the more radical anti-Federalists. The Federalists, who felt that they could win the day if given enough time to present their ideas, managed to set up an agenda that called for a separate discussion of each paragraph in the new document. As he followed these debates and spoke with Federalist leaders, Hancock found his anti-Federalist position beginning to soften. He also realized that his own influence might be decisive in the final vote. He had to consider whether he wished to be responsible for defeating the movement to create a more solid union between the states.

When Hancock returned to the convention on January 31 after a bout of illness, he had made up his mind to vote for ratification. In presenting his opinion to the delegates, he proposed nine amendments designed to curb some of the powers of the new central government. Remarkably, Sam Adams arose to indicate that he too had changed his opinion and now supported ratification. A week later, when all the discussions were over and it was time for a final vote, Hancock rose to address the delegates. His speech was remarkable for its balance, its grasp of the issues, and its faith in the future of democratic government. The proposed constitution, he said, "cannot fail to give the people of the United States a greater degree of political freedom, and eventually as much national dignity, as falls to the lot of any nation on earth." He then addressed the issue of the potential abuse of government power:

> That the [document] now to be decided upon has its defects, all agree; but when we consider the variety of interests, and the different habits of the men it is intended for, it would be very singular to have an entire union of sentiment respecting it. Were the people of the United States to delegate the powers proposed to be given, to men who were not dependent upon them frequently for elections . . . the task of delegating authority would be vastly more difficult; but as the matter now stands, the powers reserved by the people render them secure, and until they themselves become corrupt, they will always have upright and able rulers.

The vote for ratification was extremely narrow, 187 to 168, and Hancock's support clearly made the difference. Before the vote Hancock had urged all the delegates, "Let the question be decided as it may, there can be no triumph on the one side, or chagrin on the other." Recognizing the wisdom of this attitude, the anti-Federalists vowed that they would put aside their objections and work to make the new constitution a success. Hancock was given the lion's share of credit for this harmonious outcome to the debate. His popularity was higher than it had ever been, and he won reelection as governor by the highest margin he had ever enjoyed.

_____

"Let the question be decided as it may, there can be no triumph on the one side, or chagrin on the other."

_____

THE FINAL DAYS

As the new constitution was ratified and the nation prepared for its first presidential election in 1789, Hancock began to think about the possibility of national office. It was understood that the voters would choose Washington, the nation's number one hero, as the first president of the United States. However, Hancock believed that he might have a chance at being vice-president, and he allowed a number of Massachusetts newspapers to promote him as a presidential candidate. (At that time, the presidential candidate who received the second-highest number of votes became vice-president.) Hancock's name went on the ballot, but he ran a distant fifth in a field of 11, possibly because his health problems were now common knowledge. John Adams, runner-up to Washington, was to be the vice-president. Hancock was consoled by reelection to yet another term as governor, this time with Sam Adams, a staunch ally once again, as his second-in-command.

Hancock understood that he would have no more historic challenges as governor. The great issues would now be decided on the national level, and his role as a shaper of his country's destiny was at an end. During the winter of 1789–90, his health continued to decline, and his hands shook so much that he could no longer produce his legendary signature. He now spent most of his time in his room and appeared in public only on special occasions. In 1791, he felt well enough to travel, visiting New Hampshire and Connecticut, where he had considerable holdings in land, but he was never to recover his old energy. On September 18, 1793, the 56-year-old Hancock made his last appearance before the General Court; at this point he was so weak that he could neither stand up on his own nor address the legislators. On the morning of October 8, he found it difficult to catch his breath. The doctor was summoned, but in a short time Hancock was dead.

Thousands of mourners came to view Hancock's body, which lay in state at the Beacon Hill mansion for a week. The funeral, which took place on the 14th, was a magnificent affair, the greatest that Boston had ever seen. All the bells in the city

This memorial stands on Hancock's grave in Boston's Old Granary Burying Ground. John Hancock died on October 8, 1793.

tolled for an hour; every flag flew at half-mast; all the shops were closed. At 2:00 in the afternoon the massive funeral procession left Beacon Hill. There were 20,000 mourners in all, including Vice-president John Adams, a number of federal officials, everyone of note in Massachusetts, and a huge military escort. Wending its way slowly into the heart of Boston, the procession paused at the former site of the Liberty Tree, made a circuit around the State House, and proceeded to the Old Granary Burying Ground. All along the route the muffled beating of regimental drums was punctuated by the booming of cannon stationed on the hills outside the city. As Hancock's coffin was lowered into the earth, a final volley of rifle fire rang out over the cemetery.

JOHN HANCOCK'S LEGACY

In the years following his death, Hancock's reputation continued to grow. In 1812, his former enemy John Adams wrote to a friend, "I could melt into tears when I hear his name.... If benevolence, charity, generosity were ever personified in North America, they were in John Hancock." Five years later, Adams added, "I can say with truth that I profoundly admired him and more profoundly loved him. If he had vanity and caprice, so had I.... I cannot but reflect upon myself for not paying him more respect than I did in his lifetime . . . . [His talents] were far superior to many who have been much more celebrated."

It is hard to think of many figures who have played such a crucial role in American history. If Hancock is less often spoken of today than Washington, Jefferson, Franklin, or the Adamses, it is not because he contributed less. Hancock's early and steadfast opposition to British rule was a determining factor in the growth of the American Revolution. His commitment to liberty persuaded other influential figures in the colonies that the revolutionary cause was a worthy one. During the Revolutionary War, Hancock's reputation in Europe helped convince foreign powers to back the Americans. As president of the Second Continental Congress and president of the Massachusetts ratifying convention, he played a pivotal role in the creation of the two most important documents in U.S. history—the Declaration of Independence and the Constitution.

Hancock's example as a patriot was all the more powerful because he had every reason to avoid such a dangerous choice. As a wealthy and powerful merchant, Hancock could have easily paid the taxes levied by Britain, remained on good terms with the colonial authorities, and continued to fill his coffers. Hancock's enemies often charged that he became a revolutionary simply to gain popularity and become a public figure. But his admirers always believed that Hancock placed his fortune and his life in jeopardy for the sake of principle. He expressed that principle as well as anyone ever has: "I will not willingly and quietly Subject myself to Slavery." Those words have continued to echo throughout the history of the nation John Hancock did so much to create.

1737	Born John Hancock in Braintree, Massachusetts, on January 12
1744	Moves to his grandfather's house in Lexington following the death of his father
1745	Moves to Boston, where he lives with his aunt and uncle, Thomas and Lydia Hancock; begins to attend Boston Latin School
1750	Enrolls in Harvard College
1754	Receives degree from Harvard; enters his uncle's business firm
1760–61	Spends a year in London, England, conducting business for his uncle
1763	Becomes a full partner in the House of Hancock

1764	Thomas Hancock dies; John inherits the House of Hancock
1765	Hancock is elected to Boston's Board of Selectmen; British Parliament passes the Stamp Act; Bostonians organize to protest British taxation; Hancock joins in pact to boycott British imports
1766	Elected to Massachusetts legislature, the General Court
1768	British seize *Liberty,* one of Hancock's ships, as penalty for alleged smuggling; British troops are posted to Boston; Hancock is put on trial for smuggling and becomes a hero to patriots
1770	Boston Massacre takes place on March 5 as British troops fire on a mob; Hancock leads protests and is elected moderator of Boston town meeting
1772	Appointed colonel of the Boston militia
1773	Boston Tea Party takes place on December 16
1774	British pass the Coercive Acts, imposing severe restrictions on colonies; Massachusetts organizes for self-defense; First Continental Congress convenes in Philadelphia
1775	First shots of the American Revolution are fired at Lexington and Concord on

April 19; Second Continental Congress convenes in Philadelphia; Hancock is chosen president of Congress; Continental Army is founded; Battle of Bunker Hill takes place on June 17; Congress offers Olive Branch Petition to Britain; Hancock marries Dorothy Quincy; Britain rejects Olive Branch Petition

1776   Thomas Paine's *Common Sense* fuels growing call for independence; Hancock heads Marine Committee of Congress, supervising construction of Continental Navy; Congress adopts Declaration of Independence on July 4; Americans suffer military reverses in New York and New Jersey; Hancock's daughter, Lydia, is born in November

1777   Congress moves to Baltimore to avoid British threat; Hancock's infant daughter dies; British win battle of Brandywine Creek; Americans win crucial victory at Saratoga; Hancock returns to Boston

1778   Washington's troops survive brutal winter at Valley Forge; France enters into formal alliance with United States; Hancock's son, John, is born in May

1780   Hancock is elected first governor of the state of Massachusetts

1781	British forces surrender at Yorktown on October 19, assuring U.S. victory in Revolutionary War
1783	Treaty of Paris formally ends hostilities between the United States and Great Britain
1785	Hancock resigns as governor; discontent brews among Massachusetts farmers
1787	Shays's Rebellion is thwarted by Massachusetts militia; Hancock's son dies after a skating accident; Hancock is reelected governor
1788	Hancock serves as president of Massachusetts convention to vote on proposed U.S. Constitution; plays pivotal role in adoption
1789	Runs unsuccessfully in first U.S. presidential election
1793	Dies in Boston on October 8

A NOTE ON SOURCES

The bulk of the papers that John Hancock left behind are located in three Boston institutions: the New England Historic Genealogical Society, the Boston Public Library, and the Massachusetts Historical Society. Most of this material concerns Hancock's business affairs and political activities, and there are relatively few letters and documents relating to his personal life. Unlike some other revolutionary leaders—notably Thomas Jefferson, Benjamin Franklin, and John Adams— Hancock did not keep a diary and never wrote an autobiography. Historians have found additional information on his life by consulting the newspapers of the day, the writings of Hancock's contemporaries, and the records of such official bodies as the Massachusetts General Court and the Continental Congress. The first major biography of Hancock was written by Abram English Brown

(*John Hancock, His Book.* Boston: Lee & Shepard, 1898) and reproduces a number of his letters. Twentieth-century biographies include Lorenzo Sears's *John Hancock: The Picturesque Patriot* (Boston: Little Brown, 1912) and Herbert S. Allan's *John Hancock: Patriot in Purple* (New York: Beechhurst, 1953), both of which are detailed and entertaining though somewhat old-fashioned in style. The most recent narrative of Hancock's life is *The Baron of Beacon Hill* by William M. Fowler, Jr. (Boston: Houghton Mifflin, 1980). At this time, there is still no single large-scale biography of Hancock that delves deeply into all the available material.

FOR FURTHER READING

Baxter, William T. *The House of Hancock: Business in Boston, 1724–1755.* Cambridge, MA: Harvard University Press, 1945.

Berlin, Ira, and Ronald Hoffman, eds. *Slavery and Freedom in the Age of the American Revolution.* Urbana: University of Illinois Press, 1986.

Brandes, Paul D. *John Hancock's Life and Speeches: A Personalized Vision of the American Revolution.* Metuchen, NJ: Scarecrow, 1996.

Coburn, Frank. *The Battle of April 19, 1775.* Port Washington, NY: Kennicat, 1970.

Dorson, Richard M., ed. *America Rebels: Narratives of the Patriots.* New York: Pantheon, 1963.

Earle, Alice Morse. *Customs and Fashions in Old New England.* Rutland, VT: Tuttle, 1973.

Foner, Eric. *Tom Paine and Revolutionary America.* New York: Oxford University Press, 1976.

Jefferson, Thomas. *The Life and Selected Writings*

of Thomas Jefferson. Edited by Adrienne Koch and William Peden. New York: Modern Library, 1944.

Labaree, Benjamin. *The Boston Tea Party.* New York: Oxford University Press, 1964.

Maier, Pauline. *From Resistance to Revolution.* New York: Knopf, 1972.

———. *The Old Revolutionaries: Political Lives in the Age of Samuel Adams.* New York: Knopf, 1980.

Malone, Dumas. *The Story of the Declaration of Independence.* Bicentennial Edition. New York: Oxford University Press, 1975.

Middelkauff, Robert. *The Glorious Cause: The American Revolution, 1763–1789.* New York: Oxford University Press, 1982.

Purvis, Thomas L. *Revolutionary America, 1763 to 1800.* (Almanacs of American Life series.) New York: Facts On File, 1995.

Warden, G. B. *Boston, 1689–1776.* Boston: Little, Brown, 1970.

Zobel, Hiller B. *The Boston Massacre.* New York: Norton, 1970.

INDEX

Page numbers in *italics* indicate illustrations.

ABOUT THE AUTHOR

A graduate of New York University, Philip Koslow has written and edited numerous volumes for young adults, specializing in history, literature, and multicultural studies. His published works include a history of the U.S. Securities and Exchange Commission, a biography of the legendary Spanish hero El Cid, and a 12-volume series on precolonial African kingdoms. Mr. Koslow lives in Brooklyn, New York.